21 Days to a Greater You!

MS. COOKIE

21 Days to A Greater You!

Ms. Cookie

Edited: Claude R. Royston

BK Royston Publishing
P. O. Box 4321
Jeffersonville, IN 47131
502-802-5385
http://bkroystonpublishing.com
bkroystonpublishing@gmail.com

© Copyright – 2019

All Rights Reserved. No part of this book may be reproduced, stored in a retrieval system, or transmitted by any means without the written permission of the author.

Published by: BK Royston Publishing LLC
Cover Design Photo: iStockPhoto
Cover Design: Design Art

ISBN-13: 978-0692528020
ISBN-10: 0692528024
LCCN: 2015914714

Printed in the United States of America

Dedication:

I dedicate this work to everyone that desires to break old habits and create new beginnings. You can be the best and greatest individual in every endeavor that you attempt!

Cheers to a GREATER you!

Acknowledgement

To the Lover of my Soul,

I am eternally grateful for the gift of Unconditional Love and the Creative Wisdom at 3 am to pen a mini book to add value to the lives of many. I give you all the Glory, Honor, and Praise!

To My Amazing Children

"Thank you for all of the Love, Support, and Inspiration that can only come from my Young Kings and my Teeny Queen.

To My Parents,

Thank you for a greater beginning.

To my A-Team, Battle Buddies, and Host of Faithful Friends

Thank you for the late nights, the second sets of eyeballs, wiping the virtual tears, donations and believing in me!

To my Publisher and Editor

"Let's Go" is forever the marching order for this author. Thank you for assisting me and making this vision plain.

Introduction

Have you ever heard the phrases, "old habits die hard? Or old habits are hard to break?" Well there's some truth to this, however it's not impossible to break old habits and develop healthy and wholesome habits that will assist you with a greater you.

It takes 21 days for any behavior to become a habit so it's reasonable to believe that to break a habit you need to put forth a deliberate effort for at least 21 days.

It takes 21 days to create a habit. In 90 days you'll see a trend. The greater news is when you apply your new habits daily it becomes you. You want your habits to be trends that will indeed invade your life and will be recognized as your character.

If you're reading this book it means you have decided to become deliberate and intentional in your choices to make some changes in your life.

You have weighed your options and now you're creating a standard for your life that you can enjoy results that you can duplicate over and over again.

It takes 21 days to create a habit and in this book, you'll develop habits that are certain to influence your lifestyle.

I know you're ready. Get Set! Let's Go!!!

Foreword

What do you want out of life? Are there things you want to do but find yourself distracted when trying to attain those things? Do you wonder how you can reach your goals? That first step - always seems the most difficult, and not knowing what step to take can make it all the more daunting. Ms. Cookie dares to challenge you into that first step; then she will lead you to many more steps, to reach a greater, more intentional you. If there are specific things that seem to get in your way, like procrastination, Ms. Cookie will walk you out of that. If you feel a bit disorganized, Ms. Cookie will help you get things in order, for greater prioritization. This book contains daily, comprehensive steps to get you to your goals, to challenge you out of old ways of thinking, and create habits that will lead you to success, whatever that may be. This book is short, but extremely powerful. It has inspired me, and I know it will inspire you too!

~Tabitha Jackson

Do the things that will create habits that will become intentional and deliberate to a lifestyle of appreciation

Day 1 - "Who Do you Think You Are?"

This first day means everything as you embark on the journey to a greater you.
You MUST change your mindset. There are so many things we change our clothes, hair, careers, jobs but none of these are nearly as important as the priority to change your mind. The renewal of your mindset is going to set the standard of your intentions as you develop habits for a greater you.
What are you thinking right now? If it's tied to a negative past or a poor decision then you can change that at this very moment. You can make the conscious effort to seize your thoughts and transform them into something positive and beneficial for your growth.
If you're not sure what to think or even how to think here's some guidance. Think on the things that are pure, lovely, honest, noble, kind, and that bring you a sense of peace.

Day 2: "What's in your mouth?"

Let's start on day two especially since your thoughts are on the right track we want to keep this train moving along. There are two very important questions for developing this day 2 habit.

What are you saying about yourself and what do what you want to happen in your life? Your words are an amazing source of power so you want to be careful of the things you say about yourself and regarding what you'd like to see happen in your life.

The best way to speak in a way to boost your confidence is to compliment yourself. All too often we can become our own biggest critic, however it's time to pay yourself a compliment or two. You can start with an "I am" statement. You can start when you wake up every morning by saying, "I am so glad I woke up today!" Now you follow up with what you want to happen. There is an "I want" statement

And it can anything you want to see happen. You are who you say you are and you have what you say you have!

Day 3 - Time Check

Day three brings us to clock watching and waiting. The development of this habit may be a bit of a challenge if you've conditioned yourself to being impatient and antsy when you are expecting something or anything to take place. It's all a skill in learning how to wait. Timing is everything especially when a favorable outcome can be the end result. Here's a task to condition your ability to wait: choose an upscale restaurant and make arrangements to have the meal of your choice. As you are enjoying your date carefully observe the behavior of your waiter/waitress. Notice how they are waiting on you? Did you notice when you're unsure of what to order they did one of two things: asked OR gave you more time to make a selection and they allowed you the space to make a choice. Well you have that same authority in your life. Rushing and Procrastination are behaviors that DO NOT respect time. Let's eliminate those bad habits today!
Learn to wait and gain patience as a virtue.

Day 4 - Medicine for the Soul

BOL, LOL, and ROTFL are common acronyms used on social media and shorthand text to communicate a very enjoyable expression. Oh and just in case you didn't know BOL means "burst out laughing", LOL means to laugh out loud, and ROTFL means rolling on the floor laughing. Laughter does wonders for the mind and soul. Instead of crying over spilled milk you can create the habit of laughing while you clean because you can always get more milk.

Day 5 - It's Moving Day.

It's time to move. I know you're probably thinking, "Where am I going?" Well you are moving from a very dangerous place known as your comfort zone. Your comfort zone is dangerous because it's the breeding ground for mediocrity and complacency. Mediocrity and complacency are enemies to a greater you and they are not welcome in your life. So pack them up and move away! Leave no forwarding address and please don't go back to visit.

Day 6 - Phone a Friend.

Enlist your accountability partners. This is not the time for you to become an island. Solicit those you know, trust, and love to hold your feet to the fire you started to do to create productive habits. Who are you going to call? Ghostbusters is a right answer because bad habits have a way of haunting our lives much longer than we could have anticipated.

Your friend(s) will be excited that you're breaking bad habits and making greater habits. Your influence is sure to rub off on them. "No man was created to be an island; he needs some help!" ~Ms. Cookie original quote

Day 7 -Watch your diet!

Your eyes are bigger than your stomach so it's time to watch what you eat. No, not food, food. You've got to watch what you see as what you see is a method of feeding your confidence. So, watch out for the quotes and memes that are sneaky forms of self-sabotage. Your goal is to feed your faith and starve your doubts.
So those images that cause you to second guess yourself and return to your old way of thinking is junk food. It may give you a temporary boost in your emotions but the crash is imminent. Refer back to Day 1 to refresh your mindset habit.

Day 8 - Spring Cleaning

It doesn't have to be the season of spring for you to clear clutter and get organized. Now is a good time to get it done. Clear the closets, under the beds, and free your junk drawers of their misery. I like to call it a Feng shui of sorts. On this day as you de-clutter your surroundings there's a sense of peace that can flow. Organization is a great habit to develop especially as with determining and setting priorities. Everything you have in those piles that you've not used and know you won't use; donate it! Your quest to stay organized fuels the opportunity to give.

Day 9 - Have Fun

In all that we do to make the most out of any situation let's never forget to have fun. Fun is a different animal for each person but has the same outcome for all. Fun has a way of making you smile and causing expressions of enjoyment to be contagious. When you're having fun the people around you are inspired to have fun too.

Day 10 - Read!

Have you read any good books lately? Make it a point to read for 30 minutes each day. Reading is great exercise for your brain; it builds your vocabulary and enhances your ability to participate in conversations.

Elect to read books on topics that interest you. I've found it to be very relaxing to read children's books. What's your favorite children's book? Read it again and create the habit of reading a good book.

Day 11 - "The List"

There's no glory in being busy if you accomplish nothing.

Make a short "to do" list of 5 tasks. As you complete each chore place a line through that item. At the end of the day review your baby list of completed items. You may have done a lot of things in your day but you have proof that you finished five things and it feels good to see it all done.

Day 12 - Party Time

There's everything right with celebrating every success, great and small successes. There's especially something wonderful about celebrating the small successes because it means you were paying attention and taking nothing for granted. You are becoming intentional about everything and it makes a huge difference. There's nothing insignificant about your journey; everything matters. Eat some cake and dance like everybody's watching; it's your party.

Day 13 - Picture Perfect

It's said a picture is worth a 1,000 words so capture your thoughts on film. Technology presents the opportunity to have a camera available as long as you have your phone. Pictures are visuals and great reminders that beautiful things are always around you. Appreciate your surroundings. Make sure to print and keep your pictures on this page.

Day 14 - Not Too weak

Whatever you do as you are developing greater habits DO NOT GIVE UP. There are going to be days and times where the challenge will seem to be overwhelming and results are hiding. DO NOT GIVE UP. Your feelings are unreliable reporters and must be fired often. Emotions are temporary and quitting is permanent. Don't allow fleeting thoughts and moments any permanent reminders. Keep going; it gets better!

Day 15 - Buzz-Word

Okay today you're going to pick one word that you will use to inspire you EVERYTIME you say it. This one word will be the word that shapes your destiny as you say it with authority and command your day. This is a good time to get acquainted with a thesaurus to assist with choosing a word that is dynamic and gives you the extra boost you need each time you see and/ or say it. What's your one word?

Day 16 - Going places

It's time to go somewhere you've never been and see somethings you've never seen to get something you've never had and meet someone you've never met. You have the power to create opportunities and it can happen in a new environment chosen by you. It's as simple as visiting a section of your city that is not familiar to you, shopping in a store that you've never been in before. The key here enjoy the journey as much as you enjoy the destination. Take that road trip!

Day 17 - Write it down

As you continue to be intentional with these new habits is sure to chronicle your thought. Write in a journal. It's important to record your experience so that you have something on which to reflect and see your progress. You'll be very proud of your sense of accomplishment. Give yourself a gold star because you certainly deserve it.

Day 18 - Participate in and Observe growth

If you ever want to watch miracles in slow motion then plant a viable seed. This Day 18 habit is so that you have the opportunity to see firsthand the growth cycle. Make your selection of the plant of your choice. You can be as fancy or as simple as you desire. You may even choose a kit so that you have instructions and everything that you need. Plant your seeds in the dirt and water. Place your plant in the sunshine and repeat the watering routine. Don't forget to speak to your plant even when you cannot see anything. As soon as you see a sprout take a picture. Be sure to document this moment in your journal. You were a direct influence in the growth of your plant and the same applies to your own life.

Day 19 - Dear Me...

It's such a pleasure to receive mail especially when it's not associated with bad news or a bill. So this habit was inspired by the expectation of receiving not only good news but awesome adoration of a very important person: you! So ~~as~~ if you've never written a love letter before then there's no time like the present. This love letter is to yourself and even better than writing the letter you're going to mail it!

Day 20 - Random Acts

Today start the habit of making kindness count. There's no law against being kind to people even when their actions may warrant a different response. Kindness is one of those character traits that you want in abundance. So for that to happen you must make it a practice to be kind. This can be as simple as paying a compliment to someone you know or as complex as paying the debt of a random stranger. Once you have decided to be kind don't allow the negative behavior of others to distract you from your efforts.

Day 21 - It's a habit

You've made it. It's been 21 days and you've successfully created a habit. Go look in the mirror and staring back introduce yourself to a GREATER you

www.ingramcontent.com/pod-product-compliance
Lightning Source LLC
Chambersburg PA
CBHW051712090426
42736CB00013B/2663